Bullet Trains

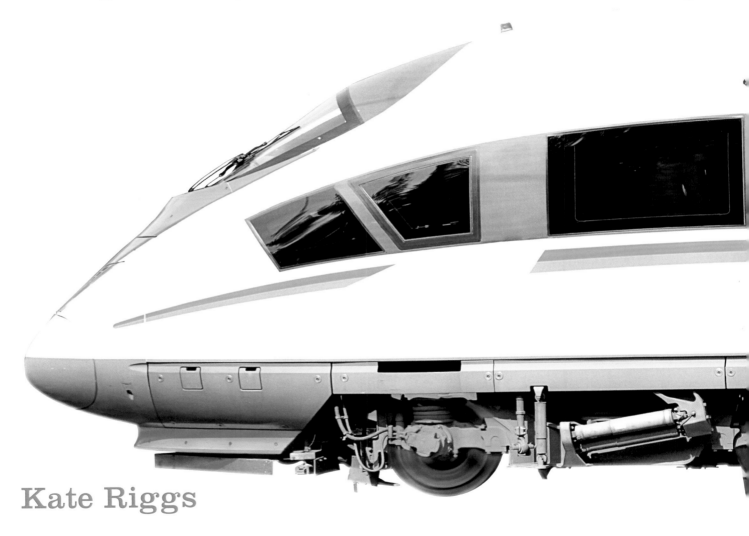

Kate Riggs

CREATIVE EDUCATION • CREATIVE PAPERBACKS

seedlings

Published by Creative Education and Creative Paperbacks
P.O. Box 227, Mankato, Minnesota 56002
Creative Education and Creative Paperbacks are
imprints of The Creative Company
www.thecreativecompany.us

Design by Ellen Huber
Production by Chelsey Luther
Printed in the United States of America

Photographs by Alamy (Prisma Bildagentur AG),
Dreamstime (Ipadimages, Dmitry Mizintsev, Potowizard,
Vacclav, Wayne0216), Getty Images (Michael Dunning,
TEH ENG KOON/AFP, xPACIFICA), Shutterstock (hxdbzxy,
mike_expert), SuperStock (age fotostock, imagebroker.net,
Photononstop, Pixtal)

Library of Congress Cataloging-in-Publication Data
Riggs, Kate.
Bullet trains / Kate Riggs.
p. cm. — (Seedlings)
Summary: A kindergarten-level introduction to bullet trains,
covering their speed, drivers, role in transportation, and
such defining features as their cars.
Includes index.
ISBN 978-1-60818-519-1 (hardcover)
ISBN 978-1-62832-119-7 (pbk)
ISBN 978-1-56660-551-9 (ebook)
1. High speed trains—Juvenile literature. I. Title. II.
Series: Seedlings.

TF1455.R45 2015
625.1—dc23   2014000180

CCSS: RI.K.1, 2, 3, 4, 5, 6, 7;
RI.1.1, 2, 3, 4, 5, 6, 7; RF.K.1, 3; RF.1.1

HC 9 8 7 6 5
PBK 9 8 7 6 5

TABLE OF CONTENTS

Time to go!

Bullet trains
are fast trains.
They take people
from place to
place.

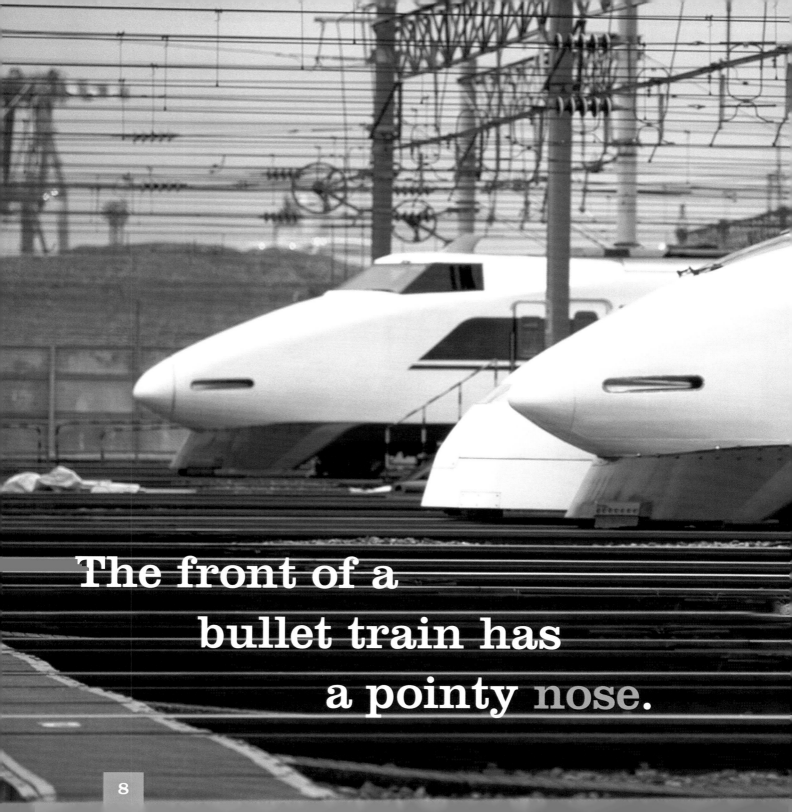

The front of a bullet train has a pointy nose.

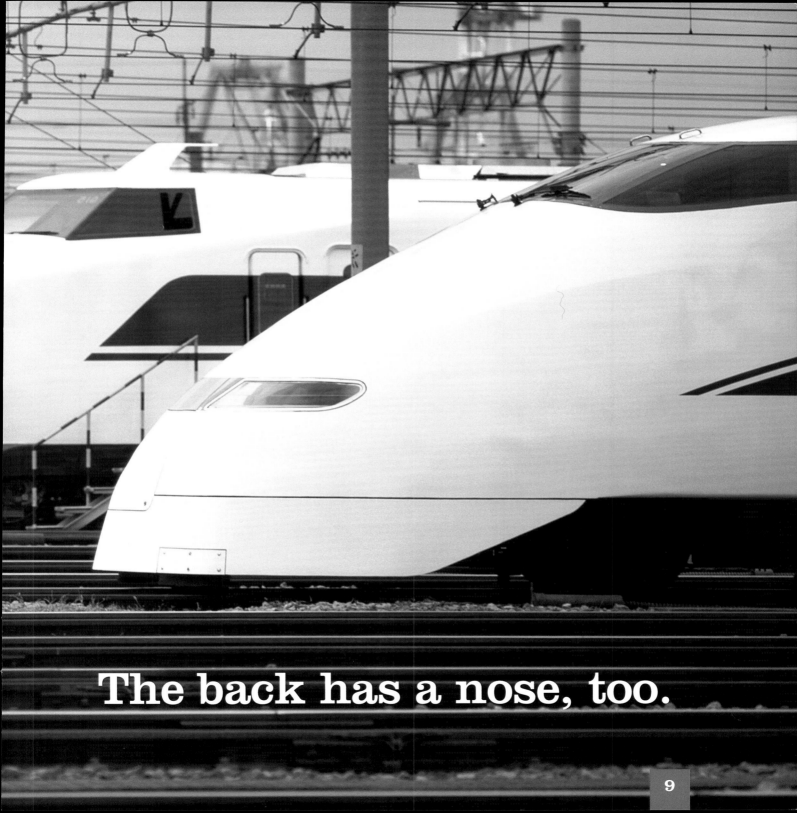

The back has a nose, too.

People ride in cars on a bullet train. Many trains have 16 cars.

Bullet trains run on smooth tracks. A **conductor** drives the train.

13

Bullet trains can go on land. They can also go underwater.

A bullet train zooms along a track. It stops at the station.

Go, bullet

train, go!

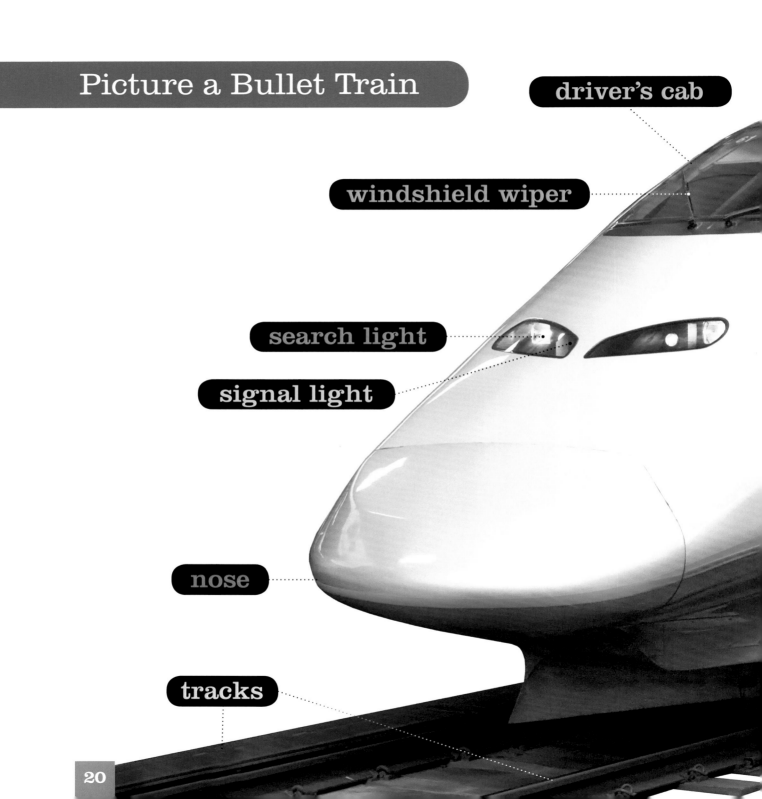

Picture a Bullet Train

driver's cab

windshield wiper

search light

signal light

nose

tracks

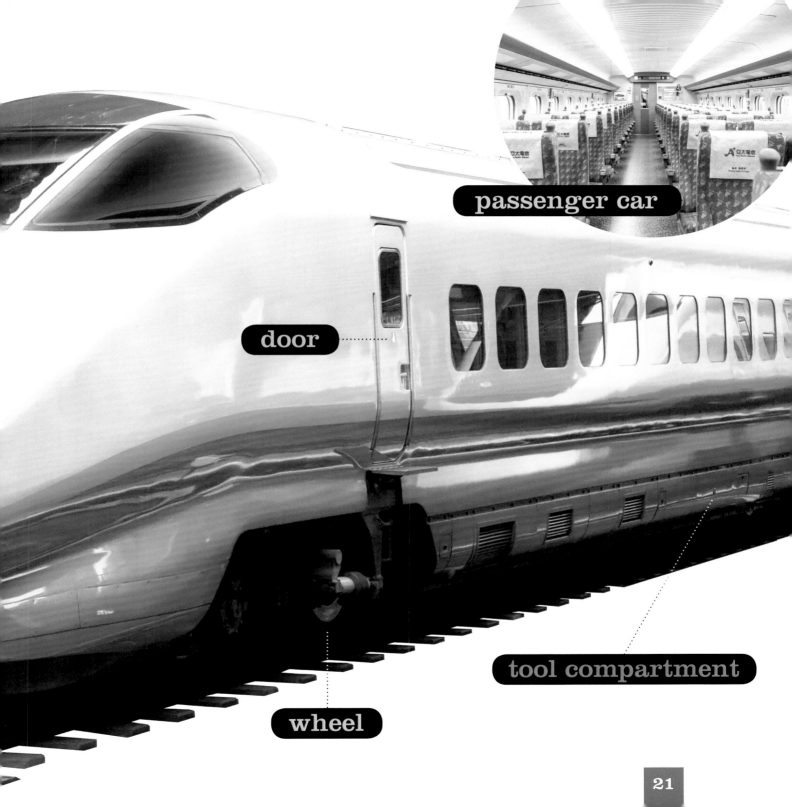

passenger car

door

wheel

tool compartment

Words to Know

cars: parts of trains where people sit

conductor: the person in charge of a train

nose: the front (or back) end of a bullet train

station: the place where trains pick up and drop off people

Read More

Balkwill, Richard. *The Best Book of Trains.*
New York: Kingfisher, 1999.

Simon, Seymour. *Seymour Simon's Book of Trains.*
New York: HarperCollins, 2002.

Websites

High-Speed Coloring Page
http://www.hellokids.com/c_15949/coloring-page
/transportation-coloring-pages/train-coloring-pages
/high-speed-coloring-page
Print out pictures of high-speed trains to color.

Train Pictures
http://discoverykids.com/articles/top-trains/
See photos of a high-speed train and other trains.

Index